Fists of Fury

Batgirl: Fists of Fury

Published by DC Comics. Cover and compilation copyright © 2004 DC Comics. All Rights Reserved. Originally published in single magazine form in BATGIRL #15, 16, 21, 26-28. Copyright © 2001, 2002 DC Comics. All Rights Reserved. All characters, their distinctive likenesses and related elements featured in this publication are trademarks of DC Comics. The stories, characters and incidents featured in this publication are entirely fictional. DC Comics does not read or accept unsolicited submissions of ideas, stories or artwork.

DC Comics, 1700 Broadway, New York, NY 10019
A Warner Bros. Entertainment Company
Printed in Canada. First Printing.
ISBN: 1-4012-0203-5
Cover art by Damion Scott & Robert Campanella
Cover color by Tom McCraw

Fists of Fury

Kelley Puckett
Scott Peterson
Writers

Damion Scott
Vincent Giarrano
Phil Noto
Pencillers

Robert Campanella
Jesse Delperdang
Inkers

Jason Wright
Gregory Wright
Colorists

John Costanza
Letterer

Damion Scott, Robert Campanella
& John Lowe
Tim Sale
Original Covers

Batman created by Bob Kane

WHO'S THAT GIRL...?

Cassandra Cain isn't a typical teenager. Her father is David Cain, an assassin whose skills are so formidable, he was once called upon to train Batman himself. David Cain passed on his voluminous knowledge of the art of combat to his only daughter. Every ounce of her energy was devoted to learning his brutal skills...even at the expense of her speech. Though trained to be the perfect assassin, Cassandra eventually decided that her father's ways were not her own. She left him and was found on the streets of Gotham by the original Batgirl, Barbara Gordon. With the blessing of Barbara, Cassandra was asked to join Batman's crusade as the new Batgirl. In the months following No Man's Land, she continued the quest for justice under Barbara's mentorship. Cassandra learned to speak with the help of a telepath, but her new verbal skills impeded her ability to read body language and thus predict her opponent's moves. The martial artist and assassin Lady Shiva helped her regain that talent, and now Batgirl is considered one of the greatest martial artists in the world.

TINK

SLIT

SZZT

EXPLAIN.

UM, WELL...

...MY INVENTION EMPLOYS A FORM OF LOW FREQUENCY MODULATION TO DIRECTLY PROPAGATE A PARTICULAR WAVEFORM ALONG THE SURFACE OF THE LOWER PREFRONTAL--

ENGLISH.

NGK! IT'S...IT MAKES YOU KILL. MAKES YOU... *DECIDE* TO KILL.

AND HAVING *DECIDED* TO KILL, THE BRAIN THEN FORMS ITS OWN SCENARIOS TO *JUSTIFY* THE KILLING, YOU SEE?

THE PRIEST'S BRAIN USED RELIGION AS AN EXCUSE. THE VETERAN'S USED WAR.

THEN... WHY *ME*?

YES, THAT... WASN'T SUCH A GOOD IDEA, WAS IT. I ASSURE YOU I DIDN'T WANT TO DIE, IT'S JUST THAT I... I DIDN'T ANTICIPATE YOUR REACTION.

YOU SEE, I'D MEANT TO *STUN* YOU--THE BEAM PUTS ONE IN A CATATONIC STATE WHILE THE BRAIN CONSTRUCTS ITS FANTASY SCENARIO.

THE VET WAS IN THAT STATE FOR TEN MINUTES BEFORE HE STARTED KILLING. FOR THE PRIEST, IT WAS AN HOUR.

BUT FOR *YOU*...

...IT WAS A *HEARTBEAT*.

DAMN, JAKE.

WHAT THE HELL'S GOING--

OH. HUH. MUST'VE BEEN HIDING.

NICE JOB, JAKE. DIDN'T THINK YOU HAD IT IN YOU.

LET'S GO, LADIES. TIME TO GET WHAT WE CAME FOR.

DEAD END.

MY DAD...

...HE'S BAD. ISN'T HE?

YES. HE IS.

BUT...YOU'RE... NOT.

OKAY?

Writer KELLEY PUCKETT

Penciller DAMION SCOTT

Inker ROBERT CAMPANELLA

Colorist JASON WRIGHT

Separator DIGITAL CHAMELEON

Letterer JOHN COSTANZA

Editor MICHAEL WRIGHT

BO-RING...

THESE ENERGY READINGS DON'T MAKE SENSE...

HEY, DID YOU PAY YOUR ELECTRIC BILL? THE LIGHTS ARE BLINKING.

I BROKE IT.

SORRY.

YOU BROKE... THE ROOM?

ORACLE, YOUR HOLO-ROOM...

SSH. BOTH OF YOU.

THERE'S SOMETHING VERY STRANGE GOING ON.

LIKE A MASSIVE ENERGY DRAIN...

UH... GUYS? GUYS?

NICE.

JEEZ... AREN'T YOU WORRIED AT ALL?

HEY, SHE'S BATGIRL.

LOOK, YOU KNOW WHAT SHE'S LIKE. SHE CAN COME BACK FROM ANYTHING.

BESIDES, SHE JUST BECAME THE FIRST PERSON IN HISTORY TO BEAT SHIVA SINGLE-HANDEDLY.

HER INJURIES AREN'T REALLY THAT SERIOUS, ALL THINGS CONSIDERED.

IT JUST... WELL, THE FIGHT TOOK A LOT OUT OF HER, PHYSICALLY, MENTALLY AND, UH, SPIRITUALLY.

SO... WHAT HAPPENED, EXACTLY?

I'M NOT SURE, THEY FOUGHT AT SOME TEMPLE DEVOTED TO THE WORSHIP OF SHIVA, AND BATGIRL WON.

OH, BUT FIRST SHIVA KILLED HER AND THEN BROUGHT HER BACK TO LIFE.

WHAT?

YEAH, THAT GOT MY ATTENTION, TOO. UNFORTUNATELY, I HAVEN'T REALLY GOTTEN MUCH MORE OUT OF--

OH...*NO*.

WHAT'S UP?

SOMETHING NOT GOOD.

...TAKE YOU TO GAZETTE SQUARE, WHERE A MAN HAS TAKEN A WOMAN HOSTAGE.

WE'RE NOT SURE WHAT HIS DEMANDS ARE AT THIS POINT...

SOMETHING NOT GOOD AT ALL.

...BUT HE'S BEEN RANTING ABOUT "THE DESTROYER OF THE DESTROYER OF WORLDS..."

"I AM BECOME DEATH, THE DESTROYER OF WORLDS."

IT'S FROM THE BHAGAVAD-GITA.

HE'S TALKING ABOUT THE ONE WHO TOOK SHIVA DOWN.

HE'S CALLING BATGIRL OUT.

OOH.

YEAH.

ALL RIGHT, WELL. GUESS I'M OFF.

WHAT? *NO.* YOU *CAN'T.* THIS GUY--

--LOOKS LIKE HE BELONGS TO THAT CULT THAT WORSHIPS SHIVA. IF HE DOES AND BATGIRL DOESN'T SHOW...

...WHO KNOWS WHAT THE REST OF THE CULT WILL DO.

EXACTLY. YOU COULD CALL IN NIGHTWING OR ROBIN, BUT THAT'D TAKE TOO LONG AND MIGHT JUST GET THE REST OF THE CULT GOING.

NOPE. IT NEEDS TO BE A FEMALE. IT'S GONNA HAVE TO BE ME.

DON'T BE SO WORRIED. I'VE GONE UP AGAINST TOUGH GUYS BEFORE.

THIS IS WHAT BATMAN TRAINED ME TO DO. PIECE O' CAKE.

SURE YOU CAN.

YEAH, RIGHT. LOOK, I'M NOT LIKE YOU-- IN FACT, NO ONE IS--

YOU JUST KINDA APPEAR IN GOTHAM ALL OF A SUDDEN, NO ONE KNOWS WHERE YOU CAME FROM, AND BOOM--

--YOU'RE THE NEW BATGIRL.

YOU'VE GOT THESE INSANE ABILITIES AND I'M NOT EVEN SURE YOU'RE NOT A METAHUMAN, AND YOU BARELY EVEN LOOK AT ME, MUCH LESS TALK...

AND NOW THIS GUY HAS A HOSTAGE AND HE'S IN A PUBLIC PLACE AND HE WANTS TO KILL ME...

...WELL, *YOU*... AND EVERY-THING'S STACKED ON HIS SIDE.

AND I TOTALLY THOUGHT I COULD TOTALLY HANDLE THIS AND NOW I'M THINKING THAT I CAN'T.

SO IF SOMETHING'S NOT WORKING, CHANGE IT. TAKE CONTROL.

MAKE IT WORK FOR YOU.

BATMAN TRUSTS YOU. ORACLE TRUSTS YOU. *YOU* JUST NEED TO TRUST YOU.

YOU CAN DO THIS.

OF COURSE.

HOW APPROPRIATE,

PLEASE,

WHAT *IS* THIS PLACE?

THE SCENE OF YOUR GREATEST TRIUMPH, OF COURSE.

IT IS WHERE I SHALL REGAIN MY HONOR.

WHEN SHIVA ENTERED THE TEMPLE, I FLED WITH THE OTHERS. I DID NOT STAND BY MY MASTER'S SIDE AS I HAD FOR SO MANY YEARS.

I TOO SHOULD HAVE WELCOMED THE GLORIOUS DEATH SHIVA WOULD BRING, AS MY MASTER DID.

SO IT WENT WELL?

 I WOULDN'T SAY THAT... BUT IT CAME OUT OKAY IN THE END.

NO MAJOR PROBLEMS, THOUGH.

 NO. NO MAJOR PROBLEMS.

 HEY... NICE JOB.

REALLY? YOU REALLY--

 --THINK--

SO.

SCOTT PETERSON
Writer
VINCENT GIARRANO
Penciller
JESSE DELPERDANG
Inker
JASON WRIGHT
Colorist
DIGITAL CHAMELEON
Separator
JOHN COSTANZA
Letterer
MICHAEL WRIGHT
Editor

CONGRATULATIONS.

I...

ALLEGED MURDERER BRUCE WAYNE STILL AT LARGE

Gotham NEWS

LET ME HELP.

I LET YOU FACE SHIVA, DESPITE THE DANGER, BECAUSE IT WAS SOMETHING YOU HAD TO DO YOURSELF.

YES. THANK YOU.

DON'T THANK ME. RETURN THE FAVOR.

SHE *BROKE* MY JAW!

NO.

YES.

NO.

YES.

NO. IF YOUR JAW WERE BROKEN, YOU WOULDN'T BE ABLE TO TALK.

AND MY LIFE WOULD BE MUCH EASIER.

NOW, GO AWAY.

I'M BUSY.

VESPER FAIRCHILD

YOU BROKE HER JAW?

NERVE STRIKE MAKES A TINY...

...FRACTURE?

RIGHT. TINY.

WELL, HIT HER HARDER NEXT TIME.

NOW, GO AWAY... I REALLY *AM* BUSY.

I SAW BATMAN.

WHAT'D HE SAY?

NOT MUCH.

"GO AWAY".

OF COURSE. DUMB QUESTION.

SO... ANY CLUES?

"CLUES"? SURE.

DOZENS OF CLUES. *HUNDREDS* OF CLUES. ROBIN, NIGHTWING AND I'VE BEEN AT IT 'ROUND THE CLOCK FOR THREE WEEKS JUST FOLLOWING ALL THE CLUES.

AND?

I *DON'T* THINK HE DID IT. I'M JUST... FOLLOWING THE EVIDENCE.

LIKE HE TAUGHT US TO.

I'M SORRY.

CAN I...DO SOMETHING?

TELL ME HE DIDN'T DO IT. AND MAKE ME BELIEVE YOU.

THAT'S IT.

THANKS.

REST IN PEACE
VESPER
KATHERINE
FAIRCHILD
OCTOBER 14, 1973 -
JANUARY 4, 2002

NOW, GO.

WHY? WHAT'RE YOU--?

WHOA. WAIT A SECOND. YOU'RE NOT THINKING WHAT I THINK YOU'RE THINKING, ARE YOU?

YOU ARE. WHY? THEY ALREADY DID THE AUTOPSY... WHY'S EVERYONE SO FREAKED-OUT ABOUT THIS BRUCE WAYNE CASE?

GO.

NO. THIS... I KNOW YOU'RE ALL DARK AND FREAKY AND STUFF, BUT THIS IS TOO WEIRD.

YOU WANT TO DIG HER UP, YOU'RE GOING TO HAVE TO KNOCK ME OUT AGAIN.

THNK

THUD

I CAN'T BELIEVE YOU DID THAT AGAIN.

I SWEAR I'M GOING TO K-

--OH, GEEZ.

NERVE STRIKE, THAT MAKES NO SENSE AT ALL.

NO, IT DOES NOT. IF YOU'RE BRUCE WAYNE AND YOU KILL VESPER IN A FIT OF RAGE, WHY WOULD YOU EVER USE A NERVE STRIKE?

BUT IF YOU'RE SETTING BRUCE WAYNE *UP,* AND YOU NEED TO GET VESPER TO WAYNE MANOR WITHOUT CHEMICALS, OR BLUNT TRAUMA, OR SIGNS OF RESTRAINT...

...YOU HIT HER WITH A NERVE STRIKE.

IF YOU KNOW *HOW.*

THIS IS GOOD.

THIS IS VERY GOOD.

HELLO? YOU OKAY?

YOU LOOK LIKE YOU COULD USE A REFILL.

NO. THANK YOU.

YES?

CONTACT.

KELLEY PUCKETT
Writer
PHIL NOTO
Penciller
ROBERT CAMPANELLA
Inker
JASON WRIGHT
Colorist
DIGITAL CHAMELEON
Separator
JOHN COSTANZA
Letterer
MICHAEL WRIGHT
Editor

114

BATGIRL.

SPOILER.

HEY. AM I... INTERRUPTING?

OH. YEAH. TRAINING. ABOUT THAT...

BATMAN WAS TRAINING ME, BUT HE'S... GONE OR SOMETHING. SO I WAS WONDERING IF... MAYBE YOU COULD SHOW ME... SOME OF *YOUR* MOVES.

NO. TOO BUSY.

WITH WHAT?

RING RING

RING RING

2 3
5 6
8 9
0 #

SO WHAT DOES SHE KNOW?

HEY.

HEY...

...WHAT'S WRONG?

NOTHING, LET'S GET STARTED.

I...

YOU WOULDN'T UNDERSTAND.

WHAT?

...NOBODY EVER TALKS ABOUT YOUR PARENTS. WHAT WAS YOUR DAD LIKE?

ASSASSIN.

DAVID CAIN.

ARE YOU SERIOUS?

YEAH.

HA HA HA

WHAT?

YOU'VE BEEN LISTENING TO ME WHINE ABOUT HAVING THE CLUEMASTER FOR A DAD, WHEN YOUR DAD'S LIKE... THE SCARIEST KILLER ON THE PLANET?

YEAH.

WHEN MY DAD WAS MAD AT ME HE'D LOCK ME IN THE CLOSET--WHAT DID YOURS DO?

SHOT ME.

HA HA HA HEH HEHH HO

OH, MAN.

I CAN'T BEAT YOU AT *ANYTHING.*

ARE YOU OKAY? WHAT HAPPENED?

IT'S... DUMB.

WELL, ACTUALLY I CAME TO TELL YOU... I WON'T BE WASTING YOUR TIME ANYMORE.

JUST WATCH... THE RIBS... OKAY?

WHAT?

YEAH, SOME... STUFF'S COME UP WITH... TIM. AND OTHER STUFF. ANYWAY, I WON'T BE AROUND AS MUCH, AND I JUST WANTED TO SAY THANKS.

KELLEY PUCKETT
Writer
DAMION SCOTT
Penciller
ROBERT CAMPANELLA
Inker
JOHN COSTANZA
Letterer
JASON WRIGHT
Colorist
DIGITAL CHAMELEON
Separator
MICHAEL WRIGHT
Editor

Covers

BATMAN
THE QUEST FOR JUSTICE CONTINUES IN THESE BOOKS FROM DC:

TO FIND MORE COLLECTED EDITIONS AND MONTHLY COMIC BOOKS FROM DC COMICS,
CALL 1-888-COMIC BOOK FOR THE NEAREST COMICS SHOP OR GO TO YOUR LOCAL BOOK STORE.

Visit us at www.dccomics.com